Computer Girl, LLC

WELCOME

"THE KEY TO WEALTH IS TO LEARN HOW TO MAKE MONEY WHILE YOU SLEEP"

J PAUL GETTY

TABLE OF CONTENTS

WHAT IS PASSIVE INCOME?

11 IDEAS TO EARN PASSIVE INCOME

SECONDARY INCOME HOW TO EARN EXTRA MONEY

FORBES TOP 10 WORK FROM HOME COMPANIES

OTHER WORK FROM HOME COMPANIES

PASSIVE INCOME

WHAT IS PASSIVE INCOME?

Passive income is income that requires little to no effort to earn and maintain. Passive income can be a great way to help you generate extra cash flow. With passive income you can have money coming in even as you pursue your primary job.

11 Ideas to Earn Passive Income

1. **Selling information products**
One popular strategy for passive income is establishing an information product, such as an eBook, or an audio or video course.

Places to publish your eBook:

- Amazon Kindle Direct Publishing (KDP)
https://kdp.amazon.com

- NOOK Press
Barnes and Noble also offers no-cost self-publishing to its NOOK e-readers
https://press.barnesandnoble.com/

- iBooks Author
If you have a Mac computer you can download the free IBook author app and and create your book using Apple's library of templates and other design tools. You can then publish your business eBook and offer it for purchase or free download in the iBooks store.

- Google Play

To make your titles available on Android devices and Google Books, there's the Google Play Books Partner Cente. The platform allows you to upload your content, set your own prices and sell to customers around the world
https://play.google.com/books/publish/u/0/

- Lulu

Lulu is a platform that lets you create and publish eBooks for a variety of different platforms and stores. You can create and format your own eBook for free, or hire Lulu to edit, proofread and design
https://www.lulu.com/

2. **Create an App**

Have you ever had an amazing idea for an app? If so, you could consider hiring a programmer to create your app for you. You could then sell it on the App store for residual income.

3. **Advertise on your car**

You may be able to earn some extra money by driving your car around. Contact a specialized advertising agency, which will evaluate your driving habits, including where you drive and how many miles. If you're a match with one of their advertisers, the agency will "wrap" your car with the ads at no cost to you. Agencies are looking for newer cars, and drivers should have a clean driving record.

4. **Create a course on Udemy**

Udemy is an online platform that lets its user take video courses on a wide array of subjects. Instead of being a consumer on Udemy you can instead be a producer, create your own video course, and allow users to purchase it. This is a fantastic option if you are highly knowledgeable in a specific subject matter

https://www.udemy.com/

5. Selling Stock Photos

Do you ever wonder where your favorite websites, blogs, and sometimes even magazines get their photos? These are normally bought from stock photo websites. If you enjoy photography you can submit your photos to stock photo sites and receive a commission every time someone purchases one of them.

Popular Stock Photo Sites

- Shutterstock
https://www.shutterstock.com/

- Dreamstime
https://www.dreamstime.com/

- Getty Images
https://www.gettyimages.com/

- istock
https://www.istockphoto.com/

- Crestock
http://www.crestock.com/

-BigStock
  https://www.bigstockphoto.com/

- Fotolia
 https://us.fotolia.com/

6. Create a Print on Demand Online Store
Print on demand allows you to sell your custom graphics on products like t-shirts, clothing, mugs, canvases, phone cases, bags, and more.

Print on Demand Companies

- Printful
Create & sell your own custom design products online with print-on-demand dropshipping.
https://www.printful.com/

- Printify
Printify is a transparent print on demand platform that makes it simple to work with multiple print providers all around the world to fulfill and send your products to your customers.
https://printify.com/

- Gooten
a globally distributed production and logistics company transforming the way online brands manufacture and fulfill merchandise to their customers
https://www.gooten.com/

- Teespring
Teespring is a print on demand platform that allows you to either create and sell products by uploading your original designs or get custom apparel for yourself or your company. Their easy to use platform makes it easy for everyone from creators to artists to make money selling their designs on loads of products.
https://teespring.com/

7. **Build your own website**

Building your own website can be a reliable source of passive income. You can sell digital or physical products. By building your own website, you gain more control over what you sell and how much money you make.

Wix
https://www.wix.com/

Squarespace
https://www.squarespace.com/

Weebly
https://www.weebly.com/

GoDaddy
https://www.godaddy.com/

Webnode
https://us.webnode.com/

8. **Create YouTube Videos**
From sponsored videos to ad revenue, you'll find that you can make recurring income from your YouTube channel. The secret to creating a successful YouTube channel is creating content on a consistent schedule for a long time.

9. **Affiliate marketing**
With affiliate marketing, website owners, social media "influencers" or bloggers promote a third party's product by including a link to the product on their site or social media account. Amazon might be the best-known affiliate partner, but eBay, Awin and ShareASale are among the larger names, too. And Instagram and TikTok have become huge platforms for those looking to grow a following and promote products.You could also consider growing an email list to draw attention to your blog or otherwise direct people to products and services that they might want.

10. **Licensing Music**
Just like stock photos you can license and earn a royalty off of your music when someone chooses to use it. Music is often licensed for YouTube Videos, commercials, and more. With the amount of YouTube videos and podcasts that are being created, there is more demand than ever for music - and people are willing to pay for it.The key way to do it is to get your music in a library that people can search a little bit of body text

11. **Run a Blog**
The most popular passive income stream tends to come from blogging. Blogging has helped countless entrepreneurs earn passive income through affiliate links, courses, sponsored posts, products, book deals, and more.

Other ways to Earn Passive Income

- Peer to Peer Lending
- Rental Properties
- Cash Back Sites
- Start a Dropshipping Store
- Invest in Stock
- Host Airbnb
- Sell Your Videos
- Help Businesses Bring in Clients
- Sell Your Stuff

Secondary Income
How to earn extra money

- Work from Home Job
- Freelance
- Online Store

eBay Store

It's now easier than ever to run an online eBay store. You can, acquire products to resell on eBay. I started selling on eBay in 2019. I sell household items, electronics clothing and more. It has been a good source for extra income. Visit my store Itsabargain81

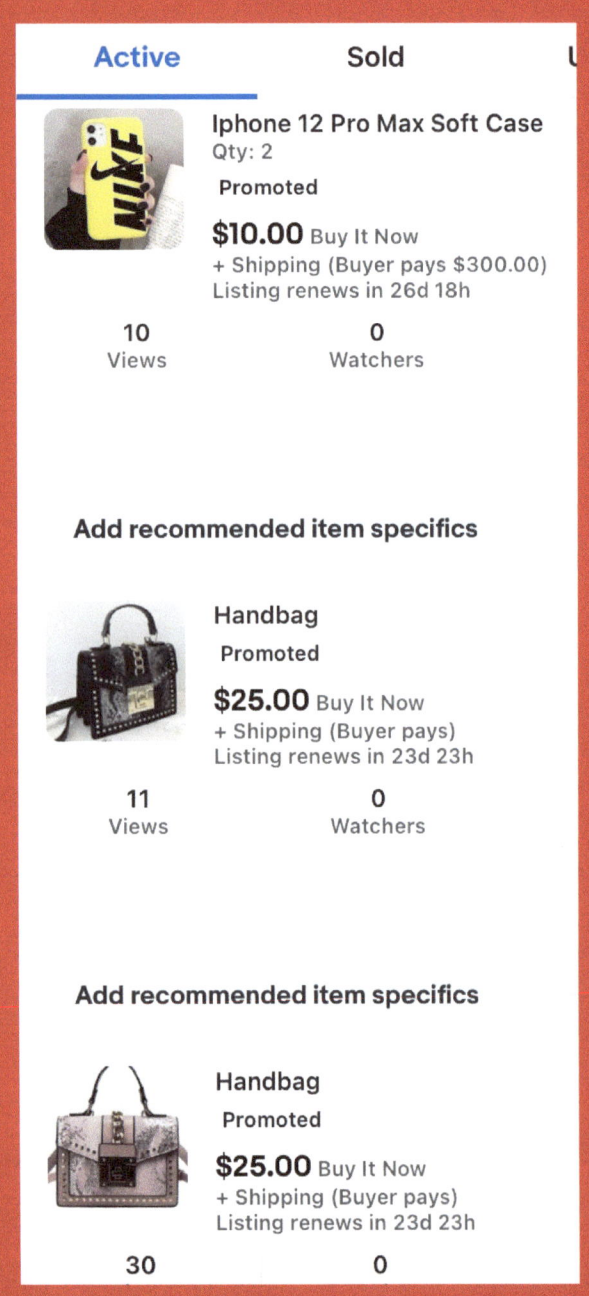
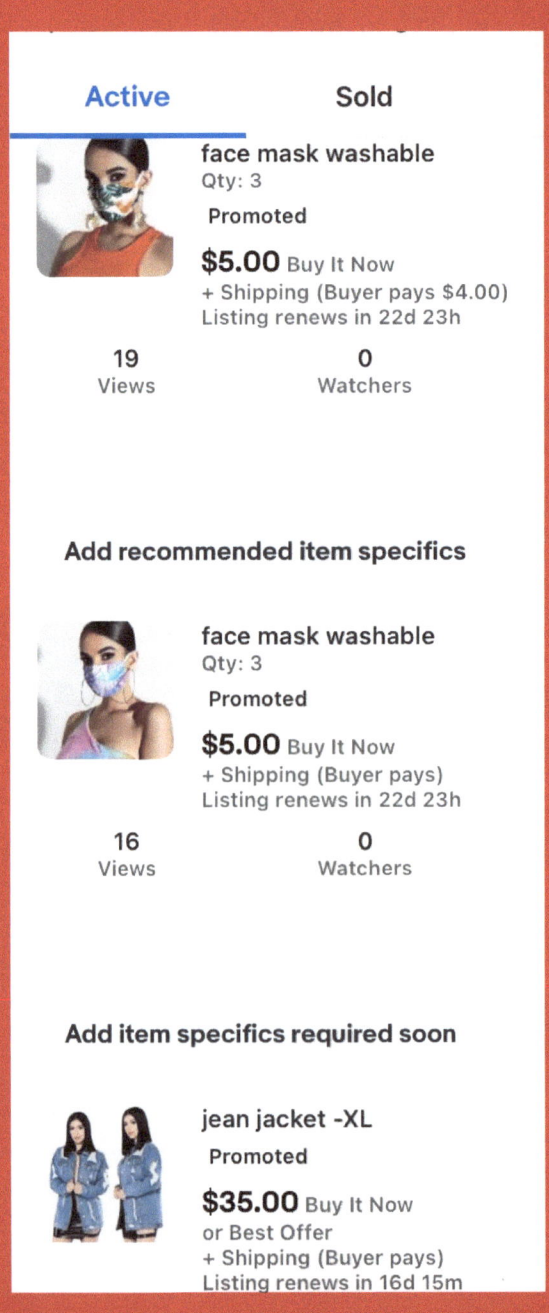

I started my eBay store with a $750.00 pallet of merchandise and tripled my money. I also sold on Amazon and Mercari APP.
https://www.mercari.com/u/262612543

It's a Bargain ✓

Welcome to our shop!
It's a Bargain Liquidation
We sell household items, small appliances, tools, b

Read more

★★★★★ 300 reviews
312 completed sales

Seller Badges ⓘ

 Member since
 Fast responder
 Quick shipper
 Reliable

All items   Hide sold items

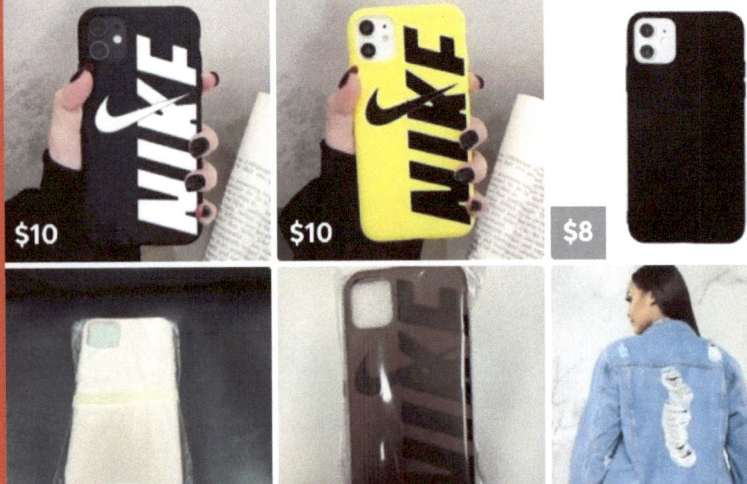

It's a Bargain

Freelance Jobs

Companies often hire freelance writers, editors, graphic designers, data-entry specialists, and more. The good thing about freelance jobs is that your hours are typically flexible – you can choose to take a job whenever you want the work and the money. You can also do most of these jobs at home.

Freelance companies

Guru
Guru.com is a freelance marketplace. It allows companies to find freelance workers for commissioned work
https://www.guru.com/

Upwork
Upwork offers tools to kickstart your freelance journey – collaborative space, built-in invoice maker, and transparent recruitment process.
https://www.upwork.com/

Fiverr

Fiverr is an Israeli online marketplace for freelance services. The company provides a platform for freelancers to offer services to customers worldwide.
https://www.fiverr.com/

Freelancer

Freelancer is a marketplace where employers and employees are able to find each other. The site allows employers to post work for site members who place bids
https://www.freelancer.com/

PART-TIME
WORK AT HOME
JOBS OPEN
NOW!

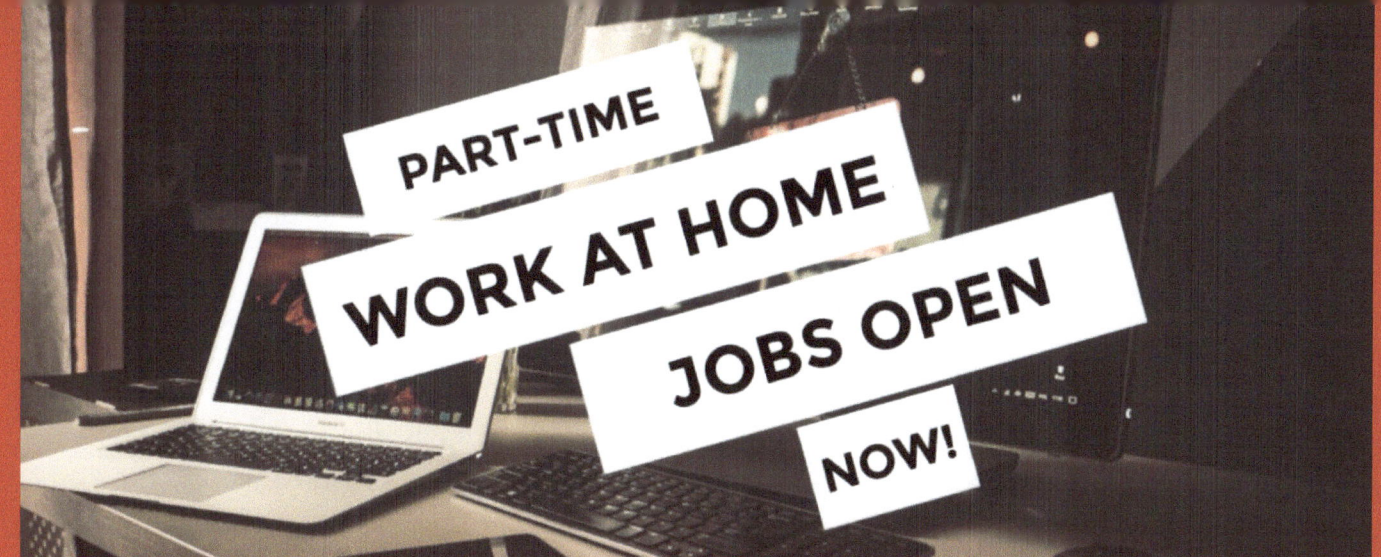

EARN SECONDARY INCOME WITH A PART-TIME WORK FROM HOME JOB

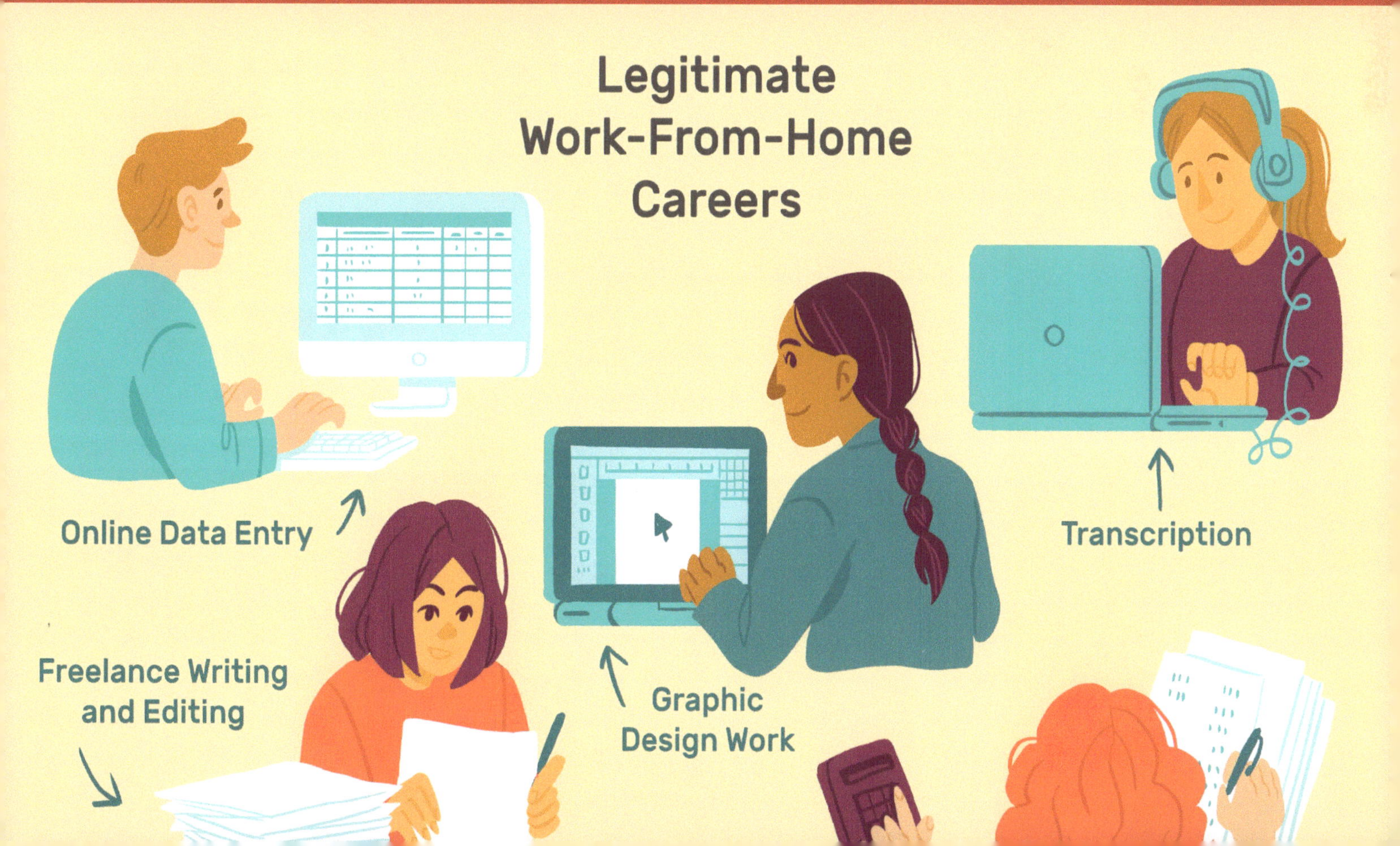
Legitimate
Work-From-Home
Careers
Online Data Entry
Transcription
Freelance Writing
and Editing
Graphic
Design Work

Forbes Top Ten Work From Home Companies

1. **Appen** is a technology services company based in Australia. However, they have offices in the US and the United Kingdom as well, and provide opportunities in 130 countries around the world. The company works with some of the biggest companies in the world, including eight of the 10 top technology companies. It supports more than 1 million contractors around the world.
http://connect.appen.com/

2. **Lionbridge** Waltham, Massachusetts-based Lionbridge has positions available that are part-time, freelance, and remote. Positions are available in banking and finance, engineering, gaming, global marketing, autos, legal services, life sciences, machine intelligence, testing, and translation and localization.
https://www.lionbridge.com/

3. **VIPKID** is based in Beijing, China, but recently opened a US headquarters in San Francisco. The company focuses on providing English language instruction. Positions are available working remotely, either part-time or freelance. The website currently advertises pay at $22 per hour. The service offers English as a second language to children in China, up to age eight.
https://www.vipkid.com/teach

4. **Liveops** Scottsdale, Arizona-based Liveops refers to itself as "The modern call center that isn't a call center". This should give you a strong indication of what they do, and how and where it takes place. The company doesn't have call centers in the usual sense, but instead employs over 20,000 independent agents, working remotely. As such, it also describes itself as the world's largest cloud contact center.
https://www.liveops.com/

5. **Working Solutions** is based in Dallas, Texas, and has been around since 1996. They provide home based customer service and sales agents. Positions are available for retail, telecommunications, finance, health care, travel, and energy. The company employees over 110,000 independent contractors from across the US.You can work full-time, part-time, or freelance, and always remotely. Positions are currently available as customer service representatives, senior living customer care, seasonal customer service agents, and customer service representatives.
https://workingsolutions.com/

6. **Amazon** Seattle based, is one of the companies most commonly associated with jobs from home. The company employs well over 90,000 workers, and is the largest online retailer in the world. You can access Amazon jobs from home on their Virtual Locations page.
https://www.amazon.jobs/en/locations/virtual-locations

7. **TTEC** Englewood, Colorado-based TTEC has been around since 1982, and is a business process outsourcing company. It provides services around the world, and operates delivery centers in 24 countries. TTEC provides work-from-home situations for consultants, customer service professionals, students, and veterans. In fact, the company employs more than 20,000 work-at-home employees. Work can involve helping customers by phone, live chat, or on the social media. Naturally, you'll be required to have Internet access and a home phone.
https://www.ttecjobs.com/

8. **Kelly Services** Founded way back in 1946, Kelly Services is one of the more well established employment agencies in the country. It's also grown to be one of the largest agencies, with almost 500,000 workers using the service worldwide. In fact, the company now provides employment opportunities in nearly 30 countries.
https://www.kellyservices.com/

9. **Concentrix** based in Freemont, California, and founded in 1983, Concentrix claims 90,000 employees worldwide. They work in a wide variety of industries, including health care, retail, transportation, e-commerce, insurance, technology, energy, and many others. Their specialties include marketing, analytics, technology, consulting, financial, and customer lifecycle management.Like many companies that offer jobs from home, Concentrix also works globally, and across dozens of different languages.
https://www.concentrix.com/

10. **United Healthcare** Healthcare providers are among the most common employers offering jobs from home. So it should be no surprise that United Healthcare is one of the top 10 companies offering work-at-home situations. Though health care typically involves hands-on work at a care facility, it also provides a surprising number of positions that can be handled remotely. https://www.uhc.com/about-us/careers

Other Work From Home Jobs

Teleperformance is hiring agents to answer calls from card members who want to redeem their reward points to book trips, travel, assist with website navigation, etc.
   Requires previous work at home experience, can multitask with good negotiating skills. Paid training with benefits. Computer provided
https://careers.teleperformanceusa.com

Custom Ink is hiring motivated individuals to review orders and assign segment information. Requires accuracy and efficiency. You must have experience with Gmail, Google Calendars, and Google Sheets. Select states only. Part-time.
https://www.customink.com/about/jobs?p=job%2FoSeGefwK

Education First is seeking people to work from home helping people learn to speak English. Work on your own schedule and use your own teaching style. Pays up to $20 per hour. Must live in the US or UK.
https://ef.com/teachonline?c=us&transaction_id=1023f8bfedd4e56476b02e600d412 5&utm_source=adbloom

Chatbooks is seeking qualified applicants to work 15 hours a week to build relationships with customers, resolve inquiries, and other duties. Requires customer service experience, be honest, a quick learner, and can type 60 wpm.
https://jobs.lever.co/chatbooks.com/

eBay is hiring reps to work from home to help eBay buyers with navigation, account setup, payments, and general questions. Requires 2 years call center or customer service experience, be a stellar communicator with a landline phone. Pays $15 per hour with benefits. Select states only.
https://jobs.ebayinc.com/search-jobs

Uhaul is hiring reps to work from home part-time assisting customers with rental rates, taking storage payments, making changes to reservations, etc. Must have a clear speaking voice with basic computer and keyboarding skills. Hourly pay with benefits.
https://jobs.uhaul.com/OpenJobs/JobDetail/R88006

Spectrum Ticketing is seeking reps to work from home selling performing arts and sports tickets on a full or part-time basis. Requires a clear speaking voice with excellent computer skills. Training provided.
https://www.spectrumticketing.com/employment

ICUC is seeking people to monitor and respond to client's social media accounts, enforce the community safety and usage policies, and encourage participation. Requires great communication and have experience with social media. Mac computers allowed.
https://jobs.smartrecruiters.com/

Magic Ears is seeking people to work from home helping kids learn to speak English.
https://t.mmears.com/v2/

Arise is a virtual call center company that has been around for a few years. You can partner with Arise as an Independent business owner. There are fees associated with this company but it is legit.
https://www.arise.com/

1800 Flowers hires temporary full-time workers to contact customers to help with their flower arrangements over the telephone. They only hire in the following states: Arizona, Delaware, Florida, Illinois, Montana, New Hampshire, New Mexico, New York, Ohio, Oklahoma, Texas, and Oregon https://www.1800flowers.com/

Officium is hiring experienced customer support reps to answer questions, report game-play software bugs, and create solutions. Must be tech-savvy, have strong verbal skills, excellent typing skills, and have a Windows 10 computer. You will work 40 hours a week. https://www.officiumlabs.io/talentplace

Hopper is hiring agents to work from home full-time to assist guests with hotel bookings. You will also help users navigate the app, troubleshoot bugs, etc. Requires 2 years experience, excellent computer skills with remote work experience. https://jobs.lever.co/hopper

Assurant has openings for agents who love helping and connecting with people to handle inbound calls from customers researching and resolving loan level inquiries in hazard insurance, mortgage banking, and property loss. Requires 1-year work experience, can multitask with good verbal skills.
https://jobs.assurant.com

Rev.com is seeking individuals to work from home adding captions to YouTube videos, educational videos, a movie, or big market brand videos. Work your own schedule. Weekly pay.
https://www.rev.com/freelancers/captions

My Employment Options has multiple work at home job openings that need to be filled. This is a free service available to those who receive SSI or SSDI disability benefits.
https://www.myemploymentoptions.com/apply-now/

Course Hero is seeking people to answer questions from students that need help in various subjects. Work your own hours. Pays $3 per answer. Hiring worldwide.
https://www.coursehero.com/

Computer Girl, LLC

www.ingramcontent.com/pod-product-compliance
Lightning Source LLC
Chambersburg PA
CBHW051820210526
45473CB00005B/1682